Polish Americans

SPIRIT
of America®

Polish AMERICANS

By Lucia Raatma

The Child's World®
Chanhassen, Minnesota

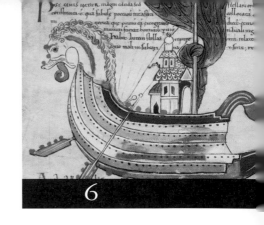

6

Polish AMERICANS

Published in the United States of America by The Child's World®
PO Box 326 • Chanhassen, MN 55317-0326 • 800-599-READ • www.childsworld.com

Acknowledgments
The Child's World®: Mary Berendes, Publishing Director

Editorial Directions, Inc.: E. Russell Primm, Emily Dolbear, Sarah E. De Capua, and Lucia Raatma, Editors; Linda S. Koutris, Photo Selector; Image Select International, Photo Research; Red Line Editorial and Pam Rosenberg, Fact Research; Tim Griffin/IndexServ, Indexer; Chad Rubel, Proofreader

Photos
Cover/frontispiece: Polish immigrants arriving in New York in 1920

Cover photographs ©: Bettmann/Corbis; Kelly-Mooney Photography/Corbis

Interior photographs ©: AKG-Images, Berlin, 6, 7 top, 7 bottom; Getty Images, 8; Corbis, 9; Getty Images, 10; Gino Domenico/AP: 11; Getty Images, 12; Getty Images, 13 top; Ann Ronan Picture Library, 13 bottom; Corbis, 14; AKG-Images, Berlin, 15 top; Corbis, 15 bottom; AKG-Images, Berlin, 16; Getty Images, 17; Corbis, 18; 19; Ann Ronan Picture Library, 20 top; Getty Images, 20 bottom; AKG-Images, Berlin, 21; Getty Images, 22, 23; Corbis, 24, Getty Images, 25 top; AFP, 25 bottom, AKG-Images, Berlin, 26 top; Corbis, 26 bottom; AKG-Images, Berlin, 27 top; Corbis, 27 bottom; Getty Images, 28 top; Corbis, 28 bottom.

Registration
The Child's World®, Spirit of America®, and their associated logos are the sole property and registered trademarks of The Child's World®.

Library of Congress Cataloging-in-Publication Data
Raatma, Lucia.
Polish Americans / by Lucia Raatma.
     v. cm.
"Spirit of America."
Includes bibliographical references and index.
Contents: Life in Poland — A new land — Making a home — The Polish American culture.
ISBN 1-56766-157-2 (lib. bdg. : alk. paper)
1. Polish Americans—Juvenile literature. [1. Polish Americans.] I. Title.
E184.P7 R32 2002
305.891'85073—dc21
                    2001007808

Contents

Chapter ONE

Life in Poland

AMONG THE FIRST EUROPEAN PEOPLE TO TRAVEL to North America were people from Poland. Some historians believe that Poles sailed with the Vikings in the 11th century. Others suggest that Poles were on the ship *Mary and Margaret*, which sailed from Germany to Jamestown, Virginia, in 1608.

An illustration of a Viking warship

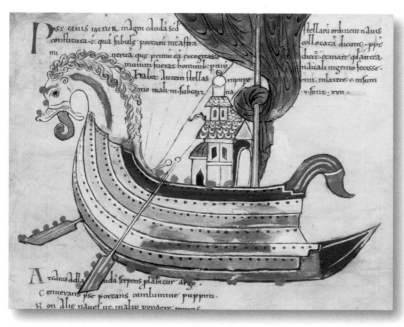

During the American Revolution (1775–1783), a number of Polish people were eager to come to America and to help in the fight for independence. Among them were Casimir Pulaski and

Tadeusz Kosciuszko. Poland had long been fighting for its own freedom, so its people sympathized with the American colonists.

For many years, the people of Poland had been controlled by governments in Russia and other countries. In 1830, the Poles rebelled against Nicholas I, the leader of Russia, in what was called the November Revolution. But Russia crushed the rebellion. Russian troops then marched into Warsaw, Poland, and many Poles were killed in the fighting. Years later, in 1863, the government of Russia began forcing their language and culture on Poland. After these incidents, many Poles fled their country. They made their way to other European cities as well as to San Francisco, New York, and Chicago in the United States.

Casimir Pulaski helped the colonists fight in the American Revolution.

Poland fighting Russia in the November Revolution

In addition to the problems with government, the Polish people suffered from poverty and lack of land. They had little hope of making a good living in Poland. So when the Poles heard stories of America, they longed to try their luck there. They heard about the **democratic** government and about the rich farmland. They heard that hard work and good ideas paid off in America.

Those Poles already in America wrote letters to their families and friends in Poland. Some offered help for others who wanted to make the journey. Some told of the great opportunities for work, and others told of the dark side—homesickness and disappointment.

In addition, a number of American companies persuaded Poles to come to work in U.S. factories and on the railroads. Many of these firms were honestly looking for good people to help in their industries.

The people of Poland struggled to make a living in their homeland.

8

Others told tall tales about high wages and wonderful jobs, which lured Poles and other Europeans to America with lies.

Young immigrants working in a glass factory in Pittsburgh, Pennsylvania

Around 1834, the first major wave of Polish **immigrants** to America began. Many of these people believed that they would stay in the United States only long enough to make a good sum of money. Then they would return to their homeland and use their new wealth to have better lives there. This plan worked for a few, but most found a new home in America and never returned to Poland.

9

A NOBLEMAN AND SOLDIER, Casimir Pulaski (right) was born in 1747 in Podolia, Poland, which is now part of Ukraine. During the 1760s and early 1770s, he and his father fought to free Poland from Russian rule, but they were unsuccessful. In 1777, he sailed to the American colonies and met with General George Washington. He offered to help Washington and the Continental Army in the Revolutionary War against Great Britain. Washington was impressed with Pulaski and encouraged Congress to make him a brigadier general.

Pulaski was an excellent leader and organized a **cavalry** called Pulaski's Legion. Pulaski and his men fought bravely and won fame throughout the colonies. While fighting the British in Savannah, Georgia, Pulaski was wounded. He died on October 11, 1779.

Years later, in honor of Casimir Pulaski's heroism, the U.S. Congress named October 11 as Pulaski Day (above). Today, in the state of Illinois, Pulaski Day is celebrated on the first Monday of March.

Chapter Two

A New Land

A Polish man preparing to board a ship headed for America

THROUGHOUT THE NINETEENTH CENTURY and into the early twentieth century, Polish immigrants came to America by the thousands. Most traveled across the Atlantic Ocean in crowded cargo ships. Their voyages on these ships often took several weeks. During that time, many passengers suffered from seasickness and diseases that spread throughout the ships. By the time they docked in New York, many immigrants were exhausted and ill.

Once in New York, newcomers were first welcomed at Castle Garden, an immigration station at the tip of Manhattan. As the number of immigrants grew, this station could not handle them all, so a new port was constructed. Starting in 1892, immigrants were processed and examined at Ellis Island in New York Harbor.

Castle Garden was the first stop for many immigrants.

Many Poles had sold most of their possessions to pay their fare to America. So when they finally arrived in the new land, they were poor and needed work. At Ellis Island, immigrants had to convince officials that they were healthy and smart enough to support themselves. The process at Ellis Island was both frightening and exciting.

Later immigrants were processed at Ellis Island.

As they settled into their new homes in America, some Poles went west and took advantage of the Homestead Act of 1862. This law gave 160 acres (65 hectares) of land to anyone willing to clear the

These Nebraska settlers received land through the Homestead Act.

land in certain western states and live on it. This gift of land appealed to many Poles. Those who wished to live in a city sought work in factories and mines in Illinois, Michigan, and Ohio. This kind of work could be very dangerous, and many Polish Americans were hurt or killed in such industries.

While many U.S. citizens realized how much immigrants could help the country, others worried about them. They feared that the newcomers could be dangerous or that they might take away jobs. Polish people quickly tried to learn English, but many were mistreated when they had trouble with the language. Some merchants overcharged Poles, realizing that the new Americans did not know the real prices of their goods.

In spite of these difficulties, Polish Americans proved to be a strong and determined people.

14

At first some moved into board-inghouses, which were fairly inexpensive places to live. As they made money, they moved into apartments and houses. Often they formed communities with other Poles and enjoyed the **camaraderie** of living with people from their homeland. Many U.S. cities soon had areas called *Polonia*—Polish-American neighborhoods.

A Polish-American family in 1940

Throughout America, Polish Americans became dressmakers and doctors, bakers and builders. Some built new Catholic churches and often sent their children to Catholic schools. The Catholic Church was very important in many Polish-American communities, and it often served as a meeting place for newcomers. Jewish Poles continued to

Many American cities have Polish communities.

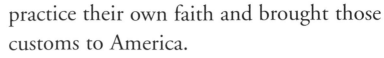

Interesting Fact

▶ During World War II, a number of Poles helped hide Jewish people from the Nazis. They risked their lives, and many were sent to concentration camps.

Adolf Hitler ordered the Nazi invasion of Poland in 1939.

practice their own faith and brought those customs to America.

During World War I (1914–1918), fewer immigrants came to America. Battles were often fought on the Atlantic Ocean, so many people chose to stay in their homeland to avoid that danger. After the war, the wave of immigrants increased once again, but in 1921 a new **quota** was enforced. Only a certain number of people from each country were allowed to enter the United States each year.

Later, more Poles came to America, but at a slower rate. When Adolf Hitler and his **Nazi** troops invaded Poland in 1939, many Poles fled. Those who escaped made their way to the United States or to other countries in Europe. And even after World War II (1939–1945), Poland continued to suffer with governmental problems. The **communist** rule imposed by Russia led many Poles to continue their **migration** to America.

A GENERAL IN THE POLISH ARMY, Tadeusz Kosciuszko (left) was born in 1746 in Poland. He was trained at military schools in both Warsaw, Poland, and Paris, France, and he served his country in its battles with Russia. In 1776, he decided to help the American colonies in their fight for freedom from British rule. Upon arriving in America, he became a colonel in the Continental army. He was skilled at building forts and planning defense. His victory during the Battle of Saratoga in New York kept the British from gaining control of the Hudson River.

After the American Revolution, Kosciuszko returned to Poland and again fought against the Russians. He was sent to prison for a time and then made his way back to America. He played a role for America in assisting France in its own revolution (1789), and he formed an important relationship with Thomas Jefferson. Kosciuszko died in 1817.

Chapter THREE

Making a Home

Milwaukee Avenue, a main street in Chicago's Polish Village

AS POLISH AMERICANS SETTLED INTO THEIR homes and neighborhoods, they often found many things to love about their new nation.

Here they had a government that allowed the people to vote (though American women did not get that right until 1920), and they had a variety of jobs to choose from. Yet Poles faced a big problem in America—a **prejudice** that went on for decades.

For reasons that are still not quite clear, many people in the United States believed that Poles were dirty, dumb, and lazy. This **stereotype** was seen in movies and on television, and many people—including well-known politicians—were known to tell jokes at the expense of Polish people.

For years, Rob Reiner (standing, left) played Mike Stivic, a character who had to endure Polish jokes made by Archie Bunker (Carroll O'Connor, seated right) on TV's All in the Family.

In spite of these attitudes, Polish Americans went on to achieve remarkable things. They embraced their history and formed Polish societies throughout America. These included the Polish National Alliance, started in 1880, and the Polish Roman Catholic Union, founded in 1873. In 1925, the Kosciuszko Foundation was begun as an organization to encourage cultural exchanges between Poland and the United States. Polish Americans fought bravely

19

Polish-American author Joseph Conrad

Lech Walesa, a union leader and later president of Poland

in both World War I and World War II, showing a love for their adopted country. Though some parts of America did not embrace the Poles, the Poles embraced America.

Over the years, a wave of Polish-American pride swept across the country. T-shirts and bumper stickers proclaimed "Polish and Proud," while public service announcements praised the accomplishments of Polish Americans including Joseph Conrad. Born Jozef Teodor Konrad Nalecz Korzeniowski, Conrad is one of the world's great writers, known for such works such as *Heart of Darkness* and *Lord Jim*.

Polish Americans watched as Lech Walesa and Solidarity, the **trade union** movement, tried to gain power in Poland during the 1980s. And they celebrated in 1978 when Cardinal Karol Wojtyla, a clergyman from Kraków, Poland, became Pope John Paul II, the leader of the Roman Catholic Church.

20

Slowly but successfully, Poles integrated themselves into the American way of life. They became police officers and elected officials. They organized schools and churches. They published newspapers and ran radio stations. Many continued to speak Polish at home while encouraging fluency in English for their children. America proved to be a place of opportunity, but it was also a land of challenge, and Polish Americans proved they could overcome the obstacles.

John Paul II, the first Polish pope in history

ON SEPTEMBER 6, 1901, AMERICA WAS dealt a terrible blow. President William McKinley (right) was **assassinated** by Leon F. Czolgosz (opposite), a Polish **anarchist**. The president had been attending the Pan American Exhibition in Buffalo, New York, when Czolgosz approached to shake his hand. But the young Pole had been hiding a gun in a handkerchief and quickly fired two shots. One bullet hit a button on McKinley's jacket, while the other hit the president in the stomach. McKinley was rushed to a nearby hospital where he died several days later. Czolgosz was found guilty of murder and executed.

The nation mourned the loss of its president, and Polish Americans found themselves hated by many citizens. More than ever, Europeans were seen as people to be feared, or at least distrusted. The assassination led to new restrictions for those wishing to come to the United States. And Poles faced more challenges in being accepted by American society.

Chapter FOUR

The Polish-American Culture

A traditional Polish wedding in Buffalo, New York

AS THE YEARS PASSED, POLISH AMERICANS worked to fight unfairness and prejudice. In the process, they made wonderful contributions to the United States.

Polish Americans are known for joyous weddings and other celebrations. Family and friends join in the fun by dancing the polka, a traditional Polish dance. Guests enjoy a wide range of Polish foods. These include *pierogi* (dumplings filled with meat, potatoes, cheese, and spices), *kielbasa* (smoked sausage), roasted chicken, cabbage, and *pierniki* (honey-spice cakes).

Polish Americans also make grand preparations for religious holidays such as Easter and Christmas.

A number of Polish Americans have become famous. Among them are baseball stars Stan Musial and Carl Yastrzemski, and ice skater Janet Lynn (Nowicki).

Ruth Handler, the youngest daughter of Polish immigrants, created Barbie, the world's most popular doll. Handler, also a cofounder of the Mattel toy company, wrote

Stan Musial of the St. Louis Cardinals

Barbie creator Ruth Handler

Interesting Fact

Stephanie Kwolek, a Polish American, invented Kevlar—an artificial material known for its high strength—in 1960 while working for the DuPont Corporation.

Nobel Prize-winning author Czeslaw Milosz

The face of Crazy Horse, a huge sculpture begun by Korczak Ziolkowski

in her autobiography, "My whole philosophy of Barbie was that through the doll, the little girl could be anything she wanted to be." Barbie and her friends, in their many different personalities, have entertained children in dozens of countries.

Polish Americans have also made many contributions to literature. Author Czeslaw Milosz wrote poems about his experiences in Warsaw during World War II and won the **Nobel Prize** for literature in 1980. Isaac Bashevis Singer wrote moving stories about his Jewish heritage in Poland and won the Nobel Prize for literature in 1978. Jerzy Kosinski has proven to be a thought-provoking writer whose works, including *Being There* and *The Painted Bird*, have been popular throughout the world.

In American art, there have been many accomplishments by Polish Americans. Polish-American sculptor Korczak Ziolkowski was a member of the team of

artists who sculpted the heads of presidents on Mt. Rushmore. He also began the huge carving of Crazy Horse in the Black Hills of South Dakota. Ziolkowski died before the project was complete, but his family has continued the work according to his plan. Ed Paschke, another Polish American, was a contemporary painter who created elaborate masks and highly stylized figures.

*Hollywood producer
Samuel Goldwyn*

In Hollywood, four Polish brothers—Jack, Harry, Sam, and Albert Warner—founded Warner Brothers Studio, while producer Samuel Goldwyn brought such notable films as *Guys and Dolls* and *The Best Years of Our Lives* to the screen. Other notable producers and directors include Joseph L. Mankiewicz and Roman Polanski. On the screen, Polish-American actors include Pola Negri, Gloria Swanson, Charles Bronson, and Stephanie Powers.

*World-renowned pianist
Artur Rubinstein*

Polish Americans have a love for a diverse range of music. Pianist Artur Rubinstein was born in Poland but moved to America when German troops invaded his country. Polish-American

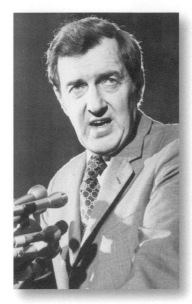

Edmund Muskie, former governor and senator from Maine

Polish Americans still enjoy dancing the polka.

singer Bobby Vinton was called the "Polish prince," and pianist Liberace entertained a variety of audiences.

In the political world, one of the best-known Polish Americans is Edmund Muskie. He served as governor of Maine and then took his place in the U.S. Senate. He ran for election as vice president with presidential candidate Hubert Humphrey in 1968, but the two lost to Richard Nixon and Spiro Agnew.

As new generations of Polish Americans are born, they continue to enrich the lives of others in the country. Yet, over the years, they run the risk of losing their Polish traditions. In America, it can be hard to live in the present while preserving the past. But today's Polish Americans have tried to do just that. They appreciate where they are, but they never forget the land of their ancestors.

1025 Boleslaw I is crowned the first king of Poland.

1500s The Polish empire reaches the height of its power.

1608 A number of Poles sail to Jamestown, Virginia, on the *Mary and Margaret.*

1776 Tadeusz Kosciuszko helps the American colonies fight for freedom.

1777 Casimir Pulaski comes to America to fight in the American Revolution.

1830 The November Revolution is crushed in Poland.

1834 Polish immigrants begin arriving in America.

1862 The Homestead Act gives 160 acres (65 hectares) of land to anyone willing to settle in certain western states.

1863 Russia imposes its language, culture, and religion on Poland.

1892 Ellis Island opens.

1901 President McKinley is assassinated by Polish anarchist Leon F. Czolgosz.

1921 A quota is set on the number of immigrants allowed into the United States per year.

1923 Warner Brothers Studio is founded by Polish brothers Harry, Albert, Sam, and Jack.

1925 The Kosciuszko Foundation is established.

1939 Adolf Hitler's Nazi troops invade Poland, causing large numbers of Poles to flee to other parts of Europe and to America.

1968 Edmund Muskie runs unsuccessfully for vice president of the United States.

1978 Cardinal Karol Wojtyla becomes Pope John Paul II.

1990 The communist government in Poland ends. Lech Walesa is elected president of the country.

1999 Poland becomes a member of the North Atlantic Treaty Organization (NATO), a military alliance of Western nations.

anarchist (AN-ar-kist)
An anarchist is someone who rebels against all authority. Leon Czolgosz, who killed President McKinley, was an anarchist.

assassinated (us-SASS-ih-nayt-ed)
Someone who has been assassinated has been murdered. President McKinley was assassinated in 1901.

camaraderie (kom-RAH-duh-ree)
Camaraderie is the show of the spirit of friendship and goodwill. Polish Americans often enjoyed the camaraderie of living near other Poles.

cavalry (KAV-ull-ree)
A cavalry is made up of soldiers who fight on horseback. Casimir Pulaski organized a cavalry called Pulaski's Legion.

communist (KOM-yuh-nist)
A communist is someone who believes in the form of government where everything is owned by the state. Poland was under communist rule after World War II.

democratic (dem-uh-KRAT-ik)
A democratic government is one where officials are elected to serve the people. In a democracy, there is equality for all people.

immigrants (IM-uh-grents)
Immigrants are people who settle in a new country. The first major wave of Polish immigrants to America occurred in 1834.

migration (mye-GRA-shun)
Migration is the movement of people from one place to another. Many Poles migrated to the U.S. to escape communism after World War II.

Nazi (NAHT-zee)
A Nazi was a person who belonged to a German group, called the Nazi party. The Nazi party was led by Adolf Hitler, who ruled Germany from 1933 to 1945. The Nazis believed that certain people and races were better than others.

Nobel Prize (noh-BEL PRIZE)
Nobel Prizes are international awards given each year for excellence in literature, economics, medicine, physics, chemistry, and for promoting peace. Czeslaw Milosz won the Nobel Prize for literature in 1980.

prejudice (PREJ-uh-diss)
A prejudice is an unfair opinion about a certain group or race. Poles have faced prejudice in America.

quota (KWOH-tuh)
A quota is a limited number. Quotas for immigration into the United States are set by the U.S. Congress.

stereotype (STER-ee-oh-tipe)
A stereotype is an oversimplified opinion of a person or group. A stereotype in the early 1900s was that Polish Americans were dumb, dirty, and lazy.

trade union (TRADE YOON-yun)
A trade union is a group that works for better conditions for workers who are members of the union. Solidarity was the name for a trade union movement in Poland during the 1980s.

For Further Information

Web Sites

Visit our homepage for lots of links about Polish Americans:
http://www.childsworld.com/links.html

Note to Parents, Teachers, and Librarians:
We routinely verify our Web links to make sure they're safe,
active sites—so encourage your readers to check them out!

Books

Bartoletti, Susan Campbell. *Dancing with Dziadziu.* New York: Harcourt Brace, 1997.

Blos, Joan W. *Brooklyn Doesn't Rhyme.* New York: Atheneum, 1994.

Estes, Eleanor. *The Hundred Dresses.* Fort Washington, Penn.: Harvest Books, 1988.

Gabor, Al. *Polish Americans.* New York: Marshall Cavendish, 1995.

Nickles, Greg. *The Poles.* New York: Crabtree Publishers, 2001.

Rollyson, Carl Sokolnicki. *A Student's Guide to Polish-American Genealogy.* Phoenix: Oryx Press, 1996.

Toor, Rachel. *The Polish Americans.* New York: Chelsea House Publishers, 1988.

Places to Visit or Contact

American Institute of Polish Culture
1440 79th Street Causeway, Suite 117
Miami, FL 33141
305-864-2349

Polish American Cultural Center
308 Walnut Street
Philadelphia, PA 19106
215-922-1700

The Polish American Museum
16 Belleview Avenue
Port Washington, NY 11050
516-883-6542

Index